MW00716609

A Pembrokeshire Album

Jean Cawood Turner

GOMER

To my family
and in memory of my parents.

First Impression—1999

ISBN 1 85902 799 7

© text and illustrations: Jean Cawood Turner

Printed in Wales at
Gomer Press, Llandysul, Ceredigion

Contents

Acknowledgements

My thanks are due to Gill Tyas for her typing skills and encouragement; to Lawrence Varney, Mayor of Newport 1991-94 and his wife Jacqueline, and also to Mike Sayko, Town Crier in the same period.

In addition I owe thanks to Terry John for reading the text and providing additional information, and to Jean Graham for checking the calendar.

Preface

During the many years that I have lived in Pembrokeshire I have been painting and recording the scenes around me as they are in the last quarter of the twentieth century. Vignettes taken from amongst those pictures form an album that I hope will give something of the flavour of this much loved county.

As a child I saw a long term calendar which fascinated me and for a long time I have wanted to devise one myself. Producing one to a manageable size has always been the problem. The solution came with this album as 'The Two Hundred Year Pembrokeshire Calendar' gradually evolved. By referring to the calendar at the back of this book, the day of the week on which events, private and public, past or future, took or will take place can be seen at a glance.

On Wednesday, the 22nd of February, 1797 the last foreign invasion of Britain took place at Carreg Wastad, Fishguard and was followed shortly by the defeat of the French force. Following the simple instructions on the calendar, it can be seen that in 1997, the 22nd of February fell on a Saturday. Fishguard celebrated this two hundredth anniversary by various events including the design and embroidery of a magnificent tapestry which remains on show.

Readers will no doubt enjoy pinpointing other historical events as well as family anniversaries, a diversion which I hope will offer as much pleasure as I have had in sharing the idea.

JT
Newport, Pembrokeshire
1999

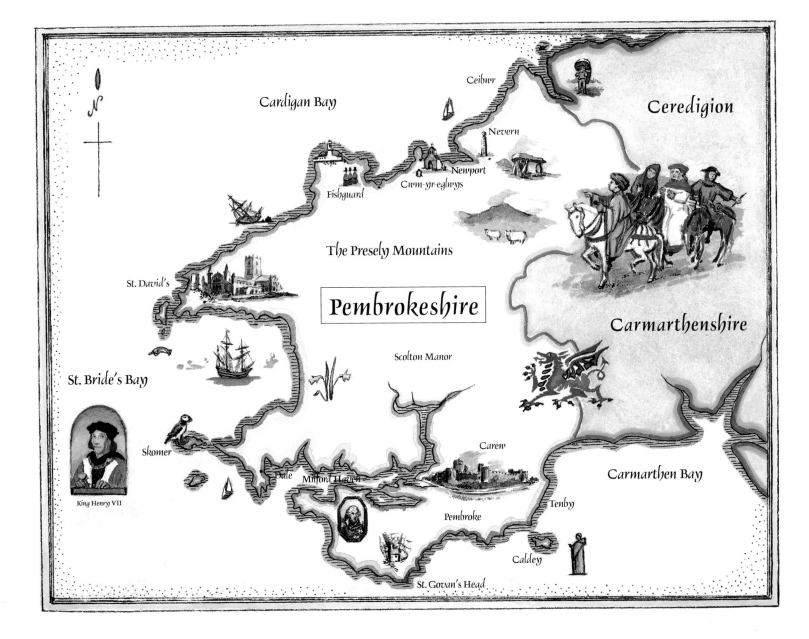

Cardigan Bay

Ceibwr

Nevern

Ceredigion

Newport

Fishguard

Cwm-yr-eglwys

The Presely Mountains

St. David's

Pembrokeshire

Carmarthenshire

Scolton Manor

St. Bride's Bay

Carew

Skomer

King Henry VII

Dale

Milford Haven

Pembroke

Carmarthen Bay

Tenby

Caldey

St. Govan's Head

Pembrokeshire, in the far west of Wales, is one of the loveliest counties of Britain's west country, and has remained one of the most unspoiled.

Bounded on three sides by the sea, Pembrokeshire boasts landscapes of infinite variety within a small compass. Reminders of its early inhabitants and fascinating history stand on every side. In the hills a Celtic enchantment seems to linger.

South Pembrokeshire, with the wonderful waterway of Milford Haven, productive land and a mild climate, was a particularly tempting target to the Normans when at the end of the 11th century with England safely under their domination, they turned acquisitive eyes towards Wales and Ireland. Needing protection for the territory they conquered, they built a number of stone castles which still stud the Pembrokeshire landscape.

Pen Dinas

Pembroke Castle

The castles form an invisible division known as 'The Landsker' between the mainly English-speaking south and the north where Welsh is the first language of many families.

Pembroke is one of the finest of Wales's mediaeval castles. Massively strong, it withstood numerous attacks by the Welsh Princes over the years. Finally, it was at the time of the Civil War that a seven-week siege headed by Cromwell himself, followed by the cutting of its water supply and the final arrival by sea of heavy siege cannon – which had been delayed by shipwreck on route from Gloucester – that forced its surrender.

The magnificent keep which stands twenty-two metres high and the strange cavern known as 'The Wogan' beneath the Great Hall are just two of the features that linger in the memory and fire the imagination.

King Henry VII
after an early 16th-century portrait from the Flemish School

Names woven into the tapestry of British history are linked with Pembroke Castle. Henry Tudor later to become King Henry VII, the founder of the resplendent Tudor dynasty was born here on the 28th January 1457. His young mother, Margaret Beaufort, Countess of Richmond was then not quite fourteen years old and newly widowed.

From a portrait of Anne Boleyn

She was being sheltered by her brother-in-law Jasper Tudor, Earl of Pembroke, whilst her husband Edmund Tudor was fighting in the Wars of the Roses.

Henry remained at Pembroke until 1471 when he and his uncle were forced to flee into exile in Brittany. In 1485 he returned to fight for the throne. When king he made his son, Henry, Earl of Pembroke. He in turn, as King Henry VIII, gave the castle to Anne Boleyn and made her Marquess of Pembroke in her own right.

Carew Castle

It was under his personal standard 'The Red Dragon of Wales' that Henry Tudor landed at Dale on his return to Pembrokeshire in 1485 to fight Richard III for the throne.

At that time Sir Rhys ap Thomas was the most powerful nobleman in Wales and owner of Carew Castle which commanded a crossing point of the river Carew. He placed his men and arms at the king's disposal. In gratitude for this help, after the victorious Battle of Bosworth Field, Henry, now King Henry VII, gave Sir Rhys gifts which enabled him to turn the castle into a home 'worthy of a Tudor gentleman'. In 1507, to celebrate having been made a Knight of the Garter, Sir Rhys hosted a splendid five-day tournament, the last Great Tournament to be held in Britain.

Manorbier Castle

The intermarriage of Norman and Welsh blood flowered with the birth, at Manorbier Castle in 1146, of Giraldus Cambrensis, Gerald the Welshman, one of Wales's greatest scholars. Gerald de Barri was the son of William de Barri, a Norman lord and Angharad, the daughter of a Norman lord and a Welsh princess, the fabulously beautiful Nest, 'The Helen of Wales'. He journeyed round Wales with Archbishop Baldwin of Canterbury recruiting for the Third Crusade. His account of these travels is said to give the best picture of life at that time. He speaks of Manorbier as 'the pleasantest spot in Wales', an opinion perhaps shared by Henry the VII, who years later granted the castle for life to his mother Margaret Beaufort, a very remarkable woman who is also remembered as the founder of St. John's College, Cambridge.

Tenby was fortified from early times and its Welsh name of Dinbych-y-Pysgod means 'Little Fort of the Fish'. The Normans built a castle here to use as a base for colonizing South Pembrokeshire.

By the end of the 13th century walls up to six metres high had been built to surround and protect the town. In the 16th century these fortifications were strengthened at a time when attack by the Spanish Armada was feared. Much of these magnificent defences survive today, including 'Five Arches' the well known Barbican-fronted gateway.

In Regency and Victorian times its beautiful beaches and fascinating maze of Mediaeval lanes had turned Tenby into a fashionable bathing resort.

The spire of St. Mary's church dominates the town. Beneath its ornate ceiling may be found the tombs of Robert Record, a Tudor mathematician who invented the equal sign, and of William Risam, a 17th-century mayor of Tenby. Risam's effigy is badly damaged. Tradition has it that during the Civil War a Cromwellian soldier mistook the figure for a lurking opponent and fired his musket at it.

Tenby Harbour

In the late 15th century an impressive house looked out over Tenby harbour. Not only was it a home but it also functioned as the business premises of someone whose work necessitated close proximity to the life of the port.

That building can still be seen in Bridge Street. Known as 'The Tudor Merchant's House', it is now in the safe keeping of the National Trust.

Carefully chosen furnishings often illustrate a practicality and dual purpose long forgotten. Original wall frescoes, together with furniture, a tiny herb garden and the delightful house itself all vividly recreate the immediate surroundings and life of its occupants.

Adjacent to the 'Tudor Mechant's House' stands the home of Charles Norris who lived and painted in Tenby at the turn of the 18th and 19th centuries. His work can be seen at Tenby Museum and gives us a unique glimpse of Pembrokeshire two hundred years ago.

Tudor Merchant's House

Caldey

It is possible to follow a footpath almost completely round the spectacular Pembrokeshire coastline. Skirting delightful little bays and wide sandy beaches it scrambles up and down over rugged cliffs where amongst the sights to see are the Stack Rocks, the Green Bridge of Wales and the Huntsman's Leap.

To the west, where the Atlantic Ocean beats against the rocks, small islands fringe the coast. Peaceful bird and wildlife sanctuaries now, their names are a reminder of a violent past when Viking raids savaged these shores: Skockholm, Grassholm, Skomer and Ramsey. The comical little puffin is amongst the birds that breed on Skomer, the largest island.

Three miles out to sea from Tenby lies Caldey, 'Cold Island'. Here a modern Cistercian priory and a 12th-century Benedictine monastery can be seen.

On the Pembrokeshire mainland, hidden at the foot of some seventy steps in a fissure in the steep cliffs of St. Govan's Head, lies a tiny chapel dedicated to the saint. It is thought to have been built in the 12th or 13th century on the site of a hermitage St. Govan established when he came over from Ireland as a Christian missionary in the 6th century.

Legend would have it otherwise, that he was in fact Sir Gawain, one of the Knights of the Round Table who, grief-stricken at King Arthur's death became a hermit. Excalibur, the King's magic sword, is said to lie at the bottom of Bosherston's lily pools nearby, which also contend as the scene of the King's demise.

Until the 18th century, these lily ponds were tidal creeks open to the sea. The Campbell family of Stackpole Court began damming the creeks one by one, thus creating a chain of fresh water lakes which are today famous for their wildlife.

St. Govan's Chapel

Around Britain there are many great houses open to the public, aristocratic homes for the most part, filled with priceless treasures. Scolton manor near Haverfordwest is of a different kind. It was the home of Pembrokeshire gentry, the Higgon family, in the Victorian/Edwardian period.

Here you will not find luxury or magnificence but a feeling of authenticity as a gracious but unpretentious way of life lives on in the architecture, furnishing and paraphernalia of that era.

Inside the house there is a costume display as well as a small art gallery. Outside, the stables and coach house contain some of the vast range of exhibits. Here there are re-creations of life in the stables, also in the carpenter's and wheelwright's workshops, a blacksmith's forge and farriery, all complete with authentic sounds.

'Margaret' at Scolton Manor

Close by, old farm implements are displayed in addition to coracles, a governess car, carts and a trap. In the open stands a preserved railway engine and a manually-operated Victorian signal box from Bancyfelin.

Sixty acres of park and woodland surround the house. Ponds, wetlands, woodlands, hedgerows and meadows are managed so as to conserve nature and yet give access for enjoyment by means of a series of nature trails.

The Visitors and Information Centre is an unusual building which shows renewable energy applications.

Scolton not only brings well-ordered and, for some, more leisured days to life but provides hours of enjoyment for visitors of all ages.

The Presely Mountains

Towards the north of Pembrokeshire run the miniature mountains or hills of Presely, now part of the National Park. Ancient tracks traverse grass and heather-covered slopes strewn with lonely boulders left behind by the Ice Age. Standing stones, stone circles, burial chambers and camps all show what importance this area once held. It is a place of mist and mystery, of fact and fiction.

It is widely believed that the 'blue stones' of the inner circle of Stonehenge in Wiltshire came from Carn Meini and Carn Alw.

Legends are woven round these hills. Merlin is said to have changed a company of knights into stone after they had mocked him. The boulders, known as Cerrig Marchogion, the Stones of the Knights, rear up in a jagged frieze on the skyline of the Presely hills and are visible for a considerable distance.

The tale of King Arthur and his knights hunting the wild boar, Y Twrch Trwyth, here is one of the ancient folk tales of the Welsh Mabinogion, but who knows, perhaps these slopes did once echo to the thud of horses' hooves and the shouts of the King's hunting party.

The river Gwaun rises on Foel Eryl, high in the Presely hills, and flows through a valley formed at the end of the Ice Age by water from thawing glaciers which cut a deep channel under the ice as it swept to meet the sea at Abergwaun or Lower Town, Fishguard.

To the north it separated the mountain of Carn Ingli from the main Presely range. Iron Age men built forts on Carn Ingli and smaller Carn Ffoi lying on its slope, both wonderful vantage points over the sea, sometimes the distant mountains of north Wales or Ireland being visible.

The lovely old Gwaun Valley is a place where ancient customs survive as if in a time warp. The New Year's Eve of the old Calendar, discontinued in 1752, is still celebrated every year on the 12th of January.

Carn Ffoi

Lower Town, Fishguard

The small harbour at Lower Town, Fishguard is very picturesque and modelled as 'Llareggyb' in the film version of Dylan Thomas's Under Milk Wood.

In 1797, Fishguard became famous as the scene of the last invasion of Britain when the French landed at Carreg Wastad. Legend has it that, by hitching up their skirts and parading in their red flannel petticoats and tall black hats, Welsh women duped the enemy into thinking they were military reinforcements.

Lower Town
from Marine Walk

This helped to bring about the French surrender which was signed at the Royal Oak Inn, Fishguard. In St Mary's churchyard there is a memorial to one Jemima Nicholas, a female cobbler dubbed 'The Pembrokeshire Heroine' who, with a pitchfork, personally rounded up twelve Frenchmen. Since 1907 Fishguard has had a large harbour at Goodwick from which the ferry plies to and from Rosslare in Ireland.

Castell Henllys

In Romano-British times merchant ships supplying the army at Hadrian's Wall put into port each night to trade and take supplies on board. Newport, on the Nevern estuary, was one such call. We know how prosperous that trade was from artefacts discovered not long ago on the site of a Romano-British farm a few miles further inland.

The farm lay close by the remains of an Iron Age hill fort, Castell Henllys, which has been the subject of an impressive reconstruction. A working loom, bedding and flickering shadows cast by a central fire help recreate the atmosphere in the largest of the surprisingly lofty and comfortable thatched huts.

The river Nevern, the sea and Carn Ingli must always have dominated the lives of all those living here. Way back in the Stone Age, men, possibly Irish settlers, built themselves a tomb looking out over all three. Of a type known as an 'Irish Channel' long cairn, Pentre Ifan cromlech is considered to be one of the best examples of a British Neolithic tomb.

Now only the massive Presely boulders that formed its skeleton loom against the sky, the enormous capstone so high that two mounted horse riders can stand beneath it, as a Victorian etching shows. Other burial chambers stand in the area, including that of Carreg Coetan Arthur.

Pentre Ifan

17

Nevern Church

The early missionaries of the 6th century brought Christianity to Wales, Ireland, Cornwall and Brittany by braving the hazards of the sea. St. Brynach founded his church at Nevern. There, on a very fine 11th-century Celtic cross in the graveyard, the first cuckoo in spring was said to sing on the 7th April, St. Brynach's Day. The cross, it is said, was being carried by St. David himself to Llanddewi Brefi. The saint was invited by St. Brynach to rest at Nevern and laid down his burden in the churchyard, where it has remained ever since.

In the avenue of ancient trees leading up to the church doors stands a tree known as 'The Bleeding Yew' which exudes a strange red sap.

By a path near the river a single cross is incised in rock where once pilgrims en route to St. David's Cathedral knelt to pray.

St. Brynach was wont to climb Carn Ingli mountain from time to time. 'To commune with the angels' the local people said. Be that as it may, that would be the reason that later it became known as Mons Angelorum.

At the foot of the mountain runs the river Nevern. For many years only stepping stones – which can still be seen – together with a rowing boat at high tide, replaced a mediaeval bridge that had once spanned the river at its lowest point. In the 16th century it had been destroyed in an attempt to contain infection that was sweeping the country. Known as 'The Sweating Sickness', it was thought to be present on Morfa headland.

St. Curig's well and chapel once stood on the southern bank of the river, close to the stepping stones and modern bridge. The waters of the well were famous for healing eye complaints. Pilgrims on their way to St. David's bathed at the well and prayed in the chapel, of which no trace now remains.

Carn Ingli

19

St. David's Cathedral

St. David, later to become the patron saint of Wales, died in 601 AD having established a Christian community on the far western tip of Pembrokeshire.

The present Cathedral was built at the end of the 12th century after previous buildings had been destroyed by Viking raids. Next to it stand the impressive remains of the Bishop's Palace built about 1340.

In the days of the great mediaeval pilgrimages, two pilgrimages to the shrine of St. David, by way of wild and dangerous roads, were considered to be of equal merit to one to Rome. Three were equivalent to one pilgrimage to the Holy Land.

It is thought that at the time of the Reformation the bones of St David, reputedly of short stature, and his companion St Justinian, said to have been tall, were hidden for safety. Bones discovered during repair work in the 19th century and answering this description now rest in a casket behind a grille in the wall of the Holy Trinity Chapel.

Also within the cathedral is the tomb of Edmund Tudor, father of King Henry VII.

Ceibwr

East of Newport Bay long stretches of cliff tower above inaccessible coves frequented by seals. The peace and solitude of one remote cove was broken in 1984 when a gang of drug smugglers constructed a secret chamber under the beach, the discovery of which led to their arrest. A little further on, the rock formations at Ceibwr Bay are particularly interesting. At Pwll-y-Wrach, the Witches' Cauldron, the roof of a cavern has collapsed to form a blow hole through which the foam spouts on stormy days.

Newport

After the Norman conquest Lordships were created within Wales and along the borders with England. Newport was one such. The Lordships held the power of a Norman Baron and a Welsh Prince but accepted the sovereignty of the King.

By the early 12th century the Normans had encroached into west Wales. Nevern Castle was built by Robert Fitz Martin as the seat of the Lordship of Cemais. His son William married Angharad, daughter of the powerful Welsh Lord Rhys. In 1191, contravening sworn oaths of peace, Rhys besieged the castle and William was ousted by his own father-in-law. Rhys was himself later imprisoned at Nevern by his sons Maelgwyn and Hywel Sais. William built himself a new castle on the slopes of Carn Ingli looking down over the Nevern estuary. The town that grew below served as the administrative capital for the Lordship of Cemais and was known as Novus Burgus.

The town still boasts its hereditary Lord or Lady Marcher. Little more than a large village, Newport is a delightful place, mainly Georgian in character, where shopping remains a sociable affair to be enjoyed rather than hurried over.

Its Welsh name, Trefdraeth, means 'town on the beach' – a hamlet said to have been submerged under sand.

Castle Street, Newport

In many parts of Pembrokeshire a rural way of life is still very much in evidence. Farm machinery may cause slow progress on the road for a while or a temporary halt be called to traffic whilst a dog helps a farmer drive a herd of cows or flock of sheep across the highway.

In parts, farms and smallholdings enjoy certain mountain rights whereby they may graze animals on the mountainside or other common land. Ponies and sheep need to be of sturdy breeds to survive winter out in the open. Winters, however, are not unduly cold and near the coast snow seldom lasts long.

With the spring comes the riot of early wild flowers for which Pembrokeshire is famous.

When the first tiny stone cottages were built they were mostly grouped in twos and threes, near water and positioned for shelter rather than to enjoy the view. Many started life as a primitive structure known as a 'Tŷ Un-nos'—'One Night Home'. Smoke issuing from the chimney of a cottage built overnight with the help of friends and neighbours established rights of tenure. The land boundaries were decided by repeatedly throwing an axe in all directions from the doorway.

Today all that remains of some are traces of crumbling walls or an animal enclosure, while others with their stout old walls make very desirable and cosy homes. A great number in Pembrokeshire bear the name of Rose Cottage – a corruption of Rhos Cottage, namely a cottage built on the common moorland.

In the National Park

Much of the beauty of Pembrokeshire is protected by the National Trust and the National Park. Where the cromlechs of the Stone Age and the boulders of Iron Age forts are set against a background of mountain and sea so much has remained the same throughout the centuries. Bees buzz in the heather, birds wheel and cry overhead and countless creatures live out their busy lives. Wind and rain may lash a monochrome landscape but then in seconds there is the sudden transformation to brilliant light and colour that is characteristic of north Pembrokeshire.

At times mist wreaths the mountain tops or drifts in from the sea to obscure or suddenly reveal the shadowy forms of rocks, trees, gorse and straggling stone walls.

Then a new dimension of mystery is added as the edges of time and reality blur in a lingering Celtic enchantment.

Today in many small towns a mayor or town crier may add colour to the local scene and ancient customs survive. Events such as a country show continue to be enjoyed. There prize cows, sheep, goats, donkeys all groomed to perfection compete for coveted rosettes. Vegetables, superb blooms, baking and brewing also vie for awards. Pony jumping and dog shows are often amongst the events taking place. Old friends are met, new ones made in the perambulation of stalls and refreshment tents; bouncy castles cater for the children and a red letter day is had by all.

Past and present, both so visible in this wonderful old county, enrich life and place the years in perspective.

Now at the close of the 20th century, poised at the start of a new millennium, we wonder what future years will bring.

In a world changing at ever increasing speed, change will be vast and unimaginable. Whatever form it takes, may the beauty of landscapes such as these survive for future generations to find in them peace, tranquility and inspiration.

Local colour

1901-2000 Anno Domini

CHART

Year	No	Year	No	Year	No	Year	No	Year	No	Year	No	Year	No	Year	No	Year	No	Year	No
1911	1	1920	12	1929	3	1938	7	1947	4	1956	8	1965	6	1974	3	1983	7	1992	11
1912	9	1921	7	1930	4	1939	1	1948	12	1957	3	1966	7	1975	4	1984	8	1993	6
1913	4	1922	1	1931	5	1940	9	1949	7	1958	4	1967	1	1976	12	1985	3	1994	7
1914	5	1923	2	1932	13	1941	4	1950	1	1959	5	1968	9	1977	7	1986	4	1995	1
1915	6	1924	10	1933	1	1942	5	1951	2	1960	13	1969	4	1978	1	1987	5	1996	9
1916	14	1925	5	1934	2	1943	6	1952	10	1961	1	1970	5	1979	2	1988	13	1997	4
1917	2	1926	6	1935	3	1944	14	1953	5	1962	2	1971	6	1980	10	1989	1	1998	5
1918	3	1927	7	1936	11	1945	2	1954	6	1963	3	1972	14	1981	5	1990	2	1999	6
1919	4	1928	8	1937	6	1946	3	1955	7	1964	11	1973	2	1982	6	1991	3	2000	14

Year	No	Year	No
1901	3	1906	2
1902	4	1907	3
1903	5	1908	11
1904	13	1909	6
1905	1	1910	7

The Pembrokeshire 200 Year Calendar

Find Year and Calendar Number in Chart and refer to calendar bearing that number

1

JANUARY	MAY	SEPTEMBER
FEBRUARY	JUNE	OCTOBER
MARCH	JULY	NOVEMBER
APRIL	AUGUST	DECEMBER

2

JANUARY	MAY	SEPTEMBER
FEBRUARY	JUNE	OCTOBER
MARCH	JULY	NOVEMBER
APRIL	AUGUST	DECEMBER

7

JANUARY	MAY	SEPTEMBER
FEBRUARY	JUNE	OCTOBER
MARCH	JULY	NOVEMBER
APRIL	AUGUST	DECEMBER

8

JANUARY	MAY	SEPTEMBER
FEBRUARY	JUNE	OCTOBER
MARCH	JULY	NOVEMBER
APRIL	AUGUST	DECEMBER

9

JANUARY	MAY	SEPTEMBER
FEBRUARY	JUNE	OCTOBER
MARCH	JULY	NOVEMBER
APRIL	AUGUST	DECEMBER

10

JANUARY	MAY	SEPTEMBER
FEBRUARY	JUNE	OCTOBER
MARCH	JULY	NOVEMBER
APRIL	AUGUST	DECEMBER

2001-2100 Anno Domini

Year	No	Year	No	Year	No	Year	No	Year	No	Year	No	Year	No	Year	No	Year	No	Year	No
2001	2	2010	6	2019	3	2028	14	2037	5	2046	2	2055	6	2064	10	2073	1	2082	5
2002	3	2011	7	2020	11	2029	2	2038	6	2047	3	2056	14	2065	5	2074	2	2083	6
2003	4	2012	8	2021	6	2030	3	2039	7	2048	11	2057	2	2066	6	2075	3	2084	14
2004	12	2013	3	2022	7	2031	4	2040	8	2049	6	2058	3	2067	8	2076	11	2085	2
2005	7	2014	4	2023	1	2032	12	2041	3	2050	7	2059	4	2068	8	2077	6	2086	3
2006	1	2015	5	2024	9	2033	7	2042	4	2051	1	2060	12	2069	3	2078	7	2087	4
2007	2	2016	13	2025	4	2034	1	2043	5	2052	9	2061	7	2070	4	2079	1	2088	12
2008	10	2017	1	2026	5	2035	2	2044	13	2053	4	2062	1	2071	5	2080	9	2089	7
2009	5	2018	2	2027	6	2036	10	2045	5	2054	5	2063	2	2072	13	2081	4	2090	1

Year	No	Year	No
2091	2	2096	8
2092	10	2097	3
2093	5	2098	4
2094	5	2099	5
2095	7	2100	6

Calendar 3 — JANUARY, MAY, SEPTEMBER; FEBRUARY, JUNE, OCTOBER; MARCH, JULY, NOVEMBER; APRIL, AUGUST, DECEMBER (S M T W T F S)

Calendar 4 — JANUARY, MAY, SEPTEMBER; FEBRUARY, JUNE, OCTOBER; MARCH, JULY, NOVEMBER; APRIL, AUGUST, DECEMBER

Calendar 5 — JANUARY, MAY, SEPTEMBER; FEBRUARY, JUNE, OCTOBER; MARCH, JULY, NOVEMBER; APRIL, AUGUST, DECEMBER

Calendar 6 — JANUARY, MAY, SEPTEMBER; FEBRUARY, JUNE, OCTOBER; MARCH, JULY, NOVEMBER; APRIL, AUGUST, DECEMBER

Calendar 11 — JANUARY, MAY, SEPTEMBER; FEBRUARY, JUNE, OCTOBER; MARCH, JULY, NOVEMBER; APRIL, AUGUST, DECEMBER

Calendar 12 — JANUARY, MAY, SEPTEMBER; FEBRUARY, JUNE, OCTOBER; MARCH, JULY, NOVEMBER; APRIL, AUGUST, DECEMBER

Calendar 13 — JANUARY, MAY, SEPTEMBER; FEBRUARY, JUNE, OCTOBER; MARCH, JULY, NOVEMBER; APRIL, AUGUST, DECEMBER

Calendar 14 — JANUARY, MAY, SEPTEMBER; FEBRUARY, JUNE, OCTOBER; MARCH, JULY, NOVEMBER; APRIL, AUGUST, DECEMBER

'The little county of Pembrokeshire is not without plenty of God's blessing as well as sufficient means for the people to live in good and plentiful sort.'

George Owen (1603)
Elizabethan historian and Lord of Cemais